Home Decor

MW00885932

25 Crazy Ideas On How To Decorate Your Home If You're Broke

Table of content

Introduction

I want to thank and congratulate you for downloading **"DIY Projects: 25 Remarkable Ideas On How to Decorate Your Home if You are Totally Broke."** You have made a good start to getting closer to decorating your home by downloading this book filled with tips and suggestions for home decorating that are affordable and simple.

There are basically hundreds of DIY decorating projects that you can do around your home. Some of these projects are quick and simple, while others can take some planning and money. If you are someone that is highly motivated and can be creative you can find ways to decorate even when you are broke. When you use your imagination to think of ways to decorate there is virtually no end to the improvements that you can make to your home.

In this book we are going to take a look at some great tips and tricks that you can use to try and make your home have that comfortable home environment that you are seeking. I hope that you will find the collection of tips and suggestions for decorating useful and beneficial in helping you to create your home sweet home!

Chapter 1 – Fixes You can Do Around Your House

Some of the things that you can do that are quick and easy fixes that can help make your quality of life better will be looked at in this chapter, along with other things that may require a bit more planning and time to achieve.

Making sure to change your grates.
When it comes to your heating grates this is something you may not give much if any thought too, but they are an important part of your HVAC system. Check your grates to see if there is any filters, they might be black foam, these are something you should replace often. To add some shine and glimmer to your home look you may consider changing the grates for something that looks more appealing such as brass grates.

Black and White Photos.
Most homes have pictures on their walls, add a simple twist by using black and white photos, they will seem more dynamic and they will make your nice picture frame stand out more.

Electric Candles.
Try using battery powered candles instead of real ones, they are less dangerous and look very similar to real candles. But with these kind of candles you do not have to worry about smoke damage and potential fires caused by an upturned candle. It will still give you that nice candlelight look in the room giving a nice ambiance.

Throws.

Often you want to do something to make your furniture look better, but you cannot afford to replace your couch at this time, so why not get a nice throw for the couch it will help to liven the old couch up without spending a fortune. You can also try adding a throw rug to cover a worn old floor.

Accent Walls.

If you cannot afford to paint the entire house, then pick accent walls instead. Pick one wall and choose a nice vibrant color this will help to make the room more dynamic looking without having to go to the expense of painting the entire room or house.

Sand and Spackle.

If you have ugly looking holes in your walls that are nothing but complete eye sores, you can get Carpenter's spackle it is cheap. It is also easy to mix and once you have applied it and allow it to dry you can then sand it down to make the offending area nice and smooth as the rest of the wall.

Light Switch Covers.

You can brighten up your home this really easy and cheap way. All you need to do is to replace your light switch covers with something that looks more appealing and eye catching. You can take off the existing covers and paint them a cool looking color. You can also do this with plug covers.

Mood Lamps.

Using lamps can help to provide a source of light, but have you ever thought of using mood lamps? You could transform a corner of a room just by adding a colored bulb. You can experiment with color without breaking the bank to do so.

Storage Ottomans.

There is nothing worse and less appealing than seeing a living room area filled with debris and clutter. Using a storage ottoman will be a nice place to store the living room clutter while also providing you with a nice place to put your feet up after a hard day at work. This is a great stylish way to get more space use out of your home.

Wall Mural Stickers.

You may think that this sounds tacky, but they actually look pretty neat. Most home improvement stores will carry wall stickers. You can use these to put wonderful patterns on your walls without knowing how to paint. They are nice and cheap and durable and you would never know that they are not done by hand unless you were inspecting them up close.

UV Paint.

If you are looking for a way to make a room truly stand out you may want to try using UV paint, it looks invisible under regular light, but when you turn on the ultraviolet lights, the paint shines with color and patterns. People have used this type of paint to create murals in UV. This is a way that you can have "normal" walls then switch them into something that looks incredible with just the flick of a switch.

Leaf Prints.

Using a leaf is a real cheap way for you to create a pattern. Some tape and good leaves, and some some spray paint to create some vibrant pattern across your walls. You could do a multicolor undercoat for leaves. Then cover and paint secondary coat, remove leaves and you will have all these multicolor leaves on your wall.

Track lighting.

Many people use track lighting for the kitchen area, they can also work in a bedroom to create different mood lighting schemes depending on how you are feeling. They can be angled to use as a reading light or just to use as a nice form of nightlight.

Shirt Sheets.

How many shirts do you have piled up in your closet and drawers? Perhaps you should try and make a colorful shirt quilt of all the shirts representing different times and experiences in your life. It will certainly be a real conversation piece while clearing out your drawers and closet giving some much needed extra space.

Box Shelves.

Take some wooden boards, that are at least a foot wide, and make them into rectangular blocks. It doesn't matter the size of them as long as they measure out to a 2:1 ratio on width and height. Now place wooden shelving inside where you feel it is needed. Take them outside and spray paint them multiple colors that will liven up a child's room. Apply a clear coat on top of this and now you have some great colorful stackable shelving that will look great. You could even add a back panel with some fun wallpaper.

Your bedroom and your family members bedrooms are special places used for having fun, falling asleep, and feeling comfortable. You can make these special spaces look fantastic just by using a few simple and inexpensive home decorating tips.

Chapter 2 – Decorating Ideas for Your Kitchen

The kitchen is an area in the home that often gets messed up, but that is okay as this means that it is a kitchen that is being well-used. But there is nothing wrong with wanting to spice your kitchen area up, without breaking the bank to do so. You can choose to give a new color and paint it, perhaps add a pot hanger to the décor. In this chapter we will offer you some ideas on how to make your kitchen look great.

Curtain Rod Drawer.

Have you ever thought what you are going to do with that unsightly looking dishtowel? Why not install a short curtain rod inside one of your cabinets. Then you can put your towel there out of sight. This will keep your towel from becoming a soggy lump on your counter top taking up valuable counter space to boot!

Chalk Wall.

This involves a bit of a process, but the end result is impressive. Invest in some blackboard paint. You usually have to put this on in several layers, but if it is applied properly you can transform a whole wall in your home into a chalk board! This would be a great thing to have in the kitchen, writing down recipes, your shopping lists. It can be fun to set up in a play room for the kids they will enjoy getting to draw on the wall.

Tin Art.

You can find all kinds of cheap art at flea markets and garage sales or thrift shops. Tin art can look really cool hanging in your kitchen.

Flowers.

Whether they are fresh or fake having colorful flowers in your home will liven the home up. It is a nice touch to have a bouquet on a table or in a window of your kitchen.

Spice Rack.

You can add a spice rack to your kitchen that will help to liven up your kitchen area. A nice looking spice rack can really make your kitchen look good plus it is so nice to have your spices within easy reach.

Paint cupboards.

Perhaps you cannot afford or simply do not want to spend thousands of dollars to replace existing kitchen cabinets. You can breath new life in to your old cabinets by painting them a new vibrant color, adding new handles to them. You will be impressed what a big difference this will make in the look of your kitchen.

Kitchen Mat.

Add a cute and colorful kitchen mat in front of your sink and see how much it will add to the look of your kitchen while helping brighten it up.

Decorative Towels.

You will be amazed how much difference a cute set of decorative towels can make in your kitchen.

There is all kinds of ways that you will be able to do in order to make your kitchen feel extra special, giving it that extra decorative boost. Just by adding your personal touch you will make your kitchen look great!

Chapter 3 – Decorating Tips for Your Bathroom

One of the most neglected areas of the average home is the bathroom. This is a room of the house that is based on function not form, but it doesn't have to be this way! In this chapter you may find some tips and suggestions that can help you to turn your bathroom into a room that will become one of your favorites within your home.

Tile Floors.
Adding some tile flooring to your bathroom does involve a bit of work, but it will be well worth the effort when you see the pleasing results. Tile is cheap and is fairly easy to install most of tile today have a self-adhering texture on the back of them.

Medicine Cabinet.
Most of the modern homes today come with a mirror and some shelving. This is a fairly inexpensive way to give yourself a new look to your bathroom space while also providing you with more storage space in your bathroom.

Curved Shower Pole.
You can increase your space within your shower just by adding a curved shower pole. This will give you more room to move around giving you the sense that your bathroom feels bigger.

Wallpaper Drawers.
Add some wallpaper to the inside of your drawers, it will look sharp adding a nice splash of color.

Coffee Can Flower Pattern.

This is a really fun trick to use when painting. Take a large coffee can and paint roughly 180 degrees, or one curved side, around it. Then move the can to the end of your line and continue it from the opposite side of can. You can create a wave pattern if done correctly.

Sponge Paints.

Try to dab paint using a sponge for a fun new look to your bathroom walls. This works really good when you use two shades of the same color. Use a section of the wall to experiment on, different sponges will give you different effects.

Grass Liner.

Use a strop of party streamer, the kind that half pre-cut frills. Tape up the solid bottom of frill upside down near bottom of wall, then spray paint, give it a once over. Remove the frill and it will look like you have a grassy field pattern along the bottom of your bathroom wall.

Candle holders.

You can spice up your bathroom by adding some candle holders to your bathroom décor. When you want to unwind from a hard day light your candles— use scented to get some aromatherapy going on, add some lavender essential oils to your tub and you have just created your own personal spa inside your bathroom!

Add a Fan Light.

Installing a fan light can help to keep the air flow moving in your bathroom to help save your paint and walls. It will also add to the overall look of your bathroom.

Mirror Art.

If you use the proper kind of paint you can make some great elegant design around the trim of your mirror adding a whole new look to you bathroom setting.

Your bathroom does not have to be a dull and boring space in your home, but unleashing your creative side can give your bathroom a whole new exciting look and feel to it at next to no cost.

Chapter 4– Decorating Tips for Your Bedroom(s)

Often the bedroom is overlooked when it comes to doing any decorating with. We should try and make some decorating improvements to important room in the home. If you have a well decorated bedroom this could mean the difference between you getting a good sleep or not. Here are some quick tips and tricks for making your bedroom a place that you will feel relaxed in.

Quilts.

Using comforters and sheets is fine, but if you really want to add that homestyle feel to your bedroom then a quilt will help you achieve this. A quilt is a work of art that you can display proudly on your bed or even on the wall of your bedroom.

New Shelves.

New shelves are actually very easy to install, and they can make your bedroom look great. You can display pictures and knick knacks on them or candles to give you a nice light for the bedroom.

Candle Mirrors.

You may want to place some mirrors across a wall in your bedroom in a certain pattern, will give a unique visual effect to your room and will also increase the lighting.

Cloud Pattern painting.

Earlier we mentioned using sponges to get a unique texture. If you are trying to give a room an open air feel consider using a blue undercoat with accents of sponge clouds. This is an easy way to liven up a room for a child and you can save money doing this yourself.

Ceiling Stars.
Another quick trick for decorating a child's room is to make their room sparkle by adding cheap ceiling stars that are easy to apply. Your kids will love staring at these cool stars lighting up their ceiling at night.

Multi-textured surfaces.
Earlier I mentioned accent walls, well consider going a bit further. Paint three walls using a base coat, then on the third wall add a different shade or wallpaper.

Stripped Furniture.
If you have old pieces of furnishings that are looking rather dull and boring, sand them down. Remove the main coat of paint and give your furnishings an unfinished, rustic look. Add a clear coat for protection, this can give your furnishings a down-home feel that can help to liven things up without spending much money.

Chapter 5 – Outdoor Home Projects

Doing the inside decorating and fixing of your home is just one part, you also have the outside of it to try and create an outdoor living space for you and your loved ones. This is a chance for you to show off your artistic flair to the outside world! In this chapter we will take a look at some decorative ideas for the outside of your home.

Trellis.

Just by adding a trellis to the outside of your home can add a new look to your house. You can choose whether you want it to be huge or paint it some eye catching colors. Decide on plants that can help add to the look of your trellis by picking plants that will grow up it such as a rose bush. Watch your trellis come to life when your plant starts to wind its way up your trellis—this beautiful work of natural art. You will gain a sense of accomplishment from doing this bit of gardening while enjoying the lovely look of your new trellis and plant.

Garden.

You may just decide that you are going to plant a garden to help to liven up the outside look of your home. You do not need to go big to have a garden. Gardens come in all shapes and sizes, there is a garden out there that will suit your needs to a tee. You might think about making a boxed garden perhaps 10×10 where you can grow your own organic veggies. Not only will this add to the outside look of your home, but it will also supply you with some fresh produce. You might like the idea of growing some tomatoes in upside down in biodegradable pouches by your trellis. You can have some real fun just designing how you are going to set things up in your garden. You can great satisfaction in growing a garden and enjoying the fruits of your labors at your dinner table each night.

Bird Bath.

Installing a bird bath in your yard in the front or backyard will draw birds and other wildlife. You can find some wonderful designs in bird baths, this will certainly add to improve the outside of your home décor. Some people go a step further than a bird bath and install a small pond, such as a fish pond.

Bird House.

This is a fun cheap hobby that you could have some real fun with designing some nice bird houses to install around your property. Paint them wonderful colors and designs.

Paint Shutters.

To help fix up the outside look of your house you can always paint the shutters of your home to give your house look a boost on the outside. Most shutters on modern homes do not really do anything. This can help you to accent the color of your home.

Sunflower Garden.

You may want to try and grow some sunflowers to add some great look and color to your property. These can act as a wonderful garden wall and when the heads start to wilt collect the heads and bake the seeds and enjoy a nice healthy treat.

Chapter 6 – Creating Your House Decorations

You can use simple crafts to make a design change in your home to perhaps suit the season. You can take a piece of existing furniture or household accessory and turn it into a piece of art as well as being a great conversation starter. It doesn't matter if your craft skills are novice or expert you will be able to create something that is going to add some charm to your home that will not cost much to do.

Interior Design Ideas:

Refurbish accessories.
One of the easiest ways to get crafty is with the crafts that you have that already exist. These can include lamp shades, table decorations, vases, lamp stands for example. You can refurbish items like these by doing them in mosaic, painting, applique art. Using materials such as wiring, fabric, and paper are just some materials that you can use to completely change the look of an accessory in your home. This will save you a lot of money because you won't have to buy new accessories for your home. By refurbishing items in your home you are updating them and possible the function that they serve may no longer what they were originally intended for. This is where your creative side can come in real handy when coming up with ideas on how to refurbish old items.

Convert unusual items in your home.
Some items we own may be no longer any use for what they were intended for originally, but if they have a cool look to them try and find a way that you can find a new use for them. You can make them into a funky looking piece of art. A great example of this is using an old window frame as a picture frame. Just create a backing that will hold your photos in place, and now you have a great looking picture frame. You may want to paint it or leave it with the old rustic look.

Display boxes made from old shoe boxes.

You can paint your old shoe boxes on the inside and outside, perhaps making some neat looking design or have them painted to match the room décor you are placing them in. You can put a nail through them and put them on the wall, great spot to display your small knick knacks. You can also use old drawers for this purpose too. You can use a hand drill to attach them to the wall, they will be able to hole heavier stuff than your shoe boxes will.

Magnetic Boards.

Having magnetic boards can be a lot of fun, you can change them as often as you want to. This can be used as a great communication tool for your family members. It is also a fun place to display pictures, that will brighten up your day when you see them, or putting up favorite quotes.

Flowers.

You can really add positive energy to your home just by adding some flowers whether they are fake or real. Adding color into a dull room through a bouquet of flowers can add some life to that boring room. Using real flowers in your home will help to leave a nice scent in the air.

Repurpose old furniture.

You can make new pieces of furniture out of the old ones. You might have an old dining room table that you could make into a nice coffee table. Just saw down the legs to coffee table size. You can also use this method to create bedside tables.

Replace the filling.

Chairs and couch cushions tend to get flattened out over time. Instead of replacing pieces of furniture just reupholster them and replace filling. If you need to get some furniture and you are on a budget check out second hand stores, flea markets and garage sales or even online at Kijiji.com often people will be giving away pieces of furniture for free.

Fabric Art.

It is amazing how a piece of the right fabric can add a real boost to the look of a room. All you need to do is to put a piece of really eye catching fabric in a picture frame, hang it up and see the difference it will make to the look of your room. You may want to try wrapping pieces of fabric around different shapes of Styrofoam stapling it to the back of them creating a nice aesthetically pleasing work of art cheap.

Carpet.

It is amazing what just a simple through rug can do to improve the look of a room. You may want to use carpet paints and paint your own personal design on a plain piece of carpet to make it unique so it blends perfectly with your room setting. It will certainly make a good conversation piece.

Recycle old glasses.

Use your old glasses as pencil holders, or use them as candle holders. Use your old teapot as a nice flower holder. You can use old jars as nice vases—paint them in all kinds of nice colors. These are great ways to decorate your home especially if you are on a low budget and you need to watch your spending. You do not have to spend a lot of money to do some home decorating. Many things for DIY decorating you will most likely already have. Making subtle changes and tweaks in your home can make a difference to how pleased you are with your home environment and the way it looks.

Enlarge Photo.

Perhaps you have an old black and white photo that you love, why not get it enlarged and put it in a picture frame so that you will be able to admire it everyday! It will add to the look of your home too!

You might be a novice at DIY decorating so you may find it a bit overwhelming at first, but you will get into it in no time at all. This will give you a chance to use your creative side while you are improving the look of your home and saving money in the process. Look around you home for items that you could fix up with a touch of paint here and there. You will be amazed how different your home will look just by adding a few inexpensive touches to it. Try and make use of what you already have in your home before you go out shopping around for more stuff. Look into old boxes and see what treasures you might find.

You might find things that with a bit of touch up can be like having new accessories in your home. Paper is the cheapest product to use and is pretty adaptable to various situations, use your creative mind. You can use paper to make seasonal items to decorate your home with. Even using wallpaper to cover other things besides walls, you could frame pieces of wallpaper to create a neat looking art piece. Use it to line your shelves or put into your bookshelves in the back. This is going to add character to your room without having to wallpaper the whole walls. It is also a great way to cut back on costs. Often you can find old wallpapers being sold in second hand stores, these are rolls that were left over from a project. You can buy them cheap and cover your bookshelves with them.

The main thing is that you can decorate your home without spending large sums of money to do so. You just need to get your creative side in working order to help you to come up with some great ideas of your own on how to refurbish items that you already have. The more things in your home that you can refurbish or touch up by giving a new coat of paint to them will save you more money in the end. The less things that you replace the less you will need to spend. So if you are truly working with a budget the best place to start looking for supplies to redo your look of your home is within your home. You will be amazed at things that you will come across and may have even forgotten about until you went hunting for new/old items to decorate your home with!

Conclusion

We have discussed a lot of different ways that you can help decorate your home inside and out without spending a large amount of money to do so. But these little improvements in your home decoration you do are going to have a huge impact on your home in a positive way. You may find that some are require too much skill, but that is the beauty of having many different ways to go about decorating your home. Who knows once you start using some of the tips and tricks offered in this book you may stumble upon some of your very own original decorating ideas!

Thanks again for downloading this book if you enjoyed it I would love it if you would leave a small review for it on Amazon it would be most helpful!

Made in the USA
Monee, IL
29 May 2022

97198248R00015